HEINEMANN GUIDE

INTERMEDIATE LEVEL
Series Editor: John Milne

The Heinemann Guided Readers provide a choice of enjoyable reading material for learners of English. The series is published at four levels. At *Intermediate Level*, the control of content and language has the following main features:

Information Control   Information which is vital to the understanding of the story is presented in an easily assimilated manner and is repeated when necessary. Difficult allusion and metaphor are avoided and cultural backgrounds are made explicit.

Structure Control   Most of the structures used in the Readers will be familiar to students who have completed an elementary course of English. Other grammatical features may occur, but their use is made clear through context and reinforcement. This ensures that the reading as well as being enjoyable provides a continual learning situation for the students. Sentences are limited in most cases to a maximum of three clauses and within sentences there is a balanced use of adverbial and adjectival phrases. Great care is taken with pronoun reference.

Vocabulary Control   There is a basic vocabulary of approximately 1,600 words. At the same time, students are given some opportunity to meet new words whose meanings are either clear from the context or are explained in the *Glossary*. Help is also given to the students in the form of illustrations which are closely related to the text.

Guided Readers at Intermediate Level

1. Shane by Jack Schaefer
2. Old Mali and the Boy by D. R. Sherman
3. A Man From Glasgow *and* Mackintosh by W. Somerset Maugham
4. Bristol Murder by Philip Prowse
5. Tales of Goha by Leslie Caplan
6. The Smuggler by Piers Plowright
7. Football by Duncan Forbes
8. The Pearl by John Steinbeck
9. Things Fall Apart by Chinua Achebe
10. The Hairless Mexican *and* The Traitor by W. Somerset Maugham
11. The Woman Who Disappeared by Philip Prowse
12. The Razor's Edge by W. Somerset Maugham
13. The Moon is Down by John Steinbeck
14. Footprints in the Jungle *and* Two Other Stories by W. Somerset Maugham
15. The Raid by Glyn Frewer
16. Scottish Adventure by Richard Chisholm
18. A Town Like Alice by Nevil Shute
19. The Queen of Death by John Milne
20. Walkabout by James Vance Marshall
21. Meet Me in Istanbul by Richard Chisholm
22. The Great Gatsby by F. Scott Fitzgerald
23. The Walker After Death by Barrie Ellis-Jones
24. The Space Invaders by Geoffrey Matthews
25. Elephant Walk by Robert Standish
26. My Cousin Rachel by Daphne du Maurier
27. The Two Million Dollar Loan by Christopher Pearson
28. Alone on the Atlantic by Monica Vincent
29. The Peacemakers by Duncan Forbes
30. I'm the King of the Castle by Susan King
31. Dracula by Bram Stoker
32. The Sign of Four by Sir Arthur Conan Doyle
33. The Speckled Band *and* Other Stories by Sir Arthur Conan Doyle

HEINEMANN GUIDED READERS
INTERMEDIATE LEVEL

W. SOMERSET MAUGHAM

The Hairless Mexican
and
The Traitor

Retold by

PHILIP KING

Illustrated by
David Knight

Heinemann International
a division of Heinemann Educational Books Ltd
Halley Court, Jordan Hill, Oxford OX2 8EJ

OXFORD   LONDON   EDINBURGH
MADRID   ATHENS   BOLOGNA
MELBOURNE   SYDNEY   AUCKLAND
IBADAN   GABORONE   NAIROBI   HARRARE
SINGAPORE   KINGSTON   PORTSMOUTH (NH)

ISBN 0 435 27009 5

'The Hairless Mexican' and 'The Traitor' were first
published by William Heinemann Ltd in 1928, in a
collection of stories entitled 'Ashenden'.

These retold versions for Heinemann Guided Readers
© Philip King 1974
This retold version first published 1974

Cover by Bill Heyes

Printed in England by Clays Ltd, St Ives plc

90 91 92 93 94 95   10 9 8

Contents

Introductory Note   vii

THE HAIRLESS MEXICAN

1. I Learn About My New Job   1
2. The Hairless Mexican   6
3. The Journey Begins   10
4. The Following Morning   12
5. The Death of the Dark Woman   15
6. Brindisi   19
7. The Search for the Papers   23
8. The Telegram   28

THE TRAITOR

1. Another Job   35
2. I Go to Lucerne   37
3. The Caypors   41
4. A Conversation with Caypor   45
5. A Lesson with Mrs Caypor   49
6. I Decide How to Act   53
7. A Walk with the Caypors   56
8. Caypor Gets a Job   61
9. Caypor in England   64

Glossary   69

A list of unsimplified books by W. Somerset Maugham can be found on page 72.

Note on Difficult Words

Some difficult words and phrases in this book are
important for understanding the story. Some of these
words are explained in the story, some are shown in the
pictures, and others are marked with a number like
this. . . .[1]. Words with a number are explained in the
glossary on page 69.

Introductory Note

The First World War began in 1914. Many countries fought in this war. The countries which interest us most in these stories are England, France, Germany, Switzerland and Italy. England and France were on one side, and Germany was on the other side. At the time of our stories, Switzerland and Italy were neutral countries. They were not fighting in the war.

The two stories in this book are both about a man called Ashenden. He did not fight as a soldier in the war, but worked as a spy for the British. A spy collects information about the enemy's plans. He tries to learn as much as possible about the enemy and gives the information to his own side.

Ashenden gave the information that he collected to a man known as 'R'. R. belonged to the British Intelligence Section. He gathered information from many spies and gave it to the British Army. Then the Army could make its plans for fighting the war.

Only a few important people knew that Ashenden was a spy. In these two stories Ashenden tells people that he is a writer. He uses the name 'Somerville', so that people will not know his real name.

GREAT BRITAIN

LONDON

DENMARK

HOLLAND

BELGIUM

GERMANY

FRANCE

BÂLE
ZÜRICH
GENEVA
SWITZERLAND

AUSTRIA

LYONS

ITALY

SPAIN

PORTUGAL

ROME

BRINDISI

NEUTRALS ━━ RAILWAYS ━━ FRONTIERS

The Hairless Mexican

1. I Learn About My New Job

My name is Ashenden and I am a writer. But during the First World War I worked as a spy for the British against the Germans. When I was a spy, I met the Hairless Mexican. He was one of the most dangerous and interesting men I have ever met. But I will begin my story at the beginning . . .

The story began in the spring of 1914. I was writing a book about Switzerland and I wanted to learn more about that country. For this reason I decided to leave England and to live in Switzerland for a year.

Some weeks before I left England, I had a visit from an old school friend. This friend explained that he was working for the Intelligence Section of the British Army.

My friend said that war was coming soon and that the chief enemy would be Germany. But Switzerland would not join in the war. Switzerland would be a neutral country, and I would be living there. Everyone would know that I was a writer. Because I was a writer, it would be easy for me to learn about the enemy's plans. Nobody would realize that I was a spy.

The result of my friend's visit was that I began to work for the Intelligence Section of the British Army.

Before I left for Switzerland, I went secretly to a large country house in the north of England. In this house, I learnt how to be a spy. I had many things to learn. One of the most difficult things was to read messages in code.

A code is like a secret language. If you write a message in code, no one can understand it unless he knows the code. This is of course very useful in war. You can send a message about the enemy's plans, and no one can read it. I had to learn several different codes.

Finally I left for Switzerland in early June. The First World War started in August.

At first my duties were very simple. Every week I sent a list of the names of Germans to London. These Germans were visiting Switzerland on their way to other countries. I had to send this list in code. I always found it very difficult to remember the correct code.

In the spring of 1915 I was given my first important job.

I received orders from London in code that I was to leave Switzerland. I was to go to a hotel in Lyons in France. I would meet the chief of the Intelligence Section in this hotel. No one knew his real name. Everyone knew him simply as 'R'. I realized this job must be very important because R. himself was coming to meet me.

My orders told me to go to the Hotel Splendide in Lyons. In the Hotel Splendide I was to make sure that I got into room number twenty-five. I was to wait in room number twenty-five for someone to knock at the door. This person would ask if he could borrow an English newspaper. Then I would know that this person was R.

I got to Lyons in the afternoon and went to the Hotel Splendide. I asked for room number twenty-five, which was empty. I made myself comfortable in the room and started to read an exciting book. Some time later I heard a knock at the door. I opened the door and a well-dressed Englishman was standing there.

'Excuse me,' he said, 'have you got an English newspaper that I can borrow?'

I realized that this gentleman must be R. I asked him to come in.

R. came into the room. He did not sit down at once. He walked slowly around the room. When he came to the curtains, he opened them a little and looked carefully through the window.

'I thought perhaps somebody had followed me,' he said to me. 'But I can't see anyone outside. Still, I don't want to take any chances.'

He looked at me and sat down. There was a smile on his lips, but his eyes were cold and serious. I knew that he was thinking about the job that he wanted me to do.

There was silence for two or three minutes and then he spoke to me.

'A man is coming here to see us tonight,' R. said. 'He will be here about eleven.' R. looked at his watch. It was half past ten. The man would come in half an hour.

'This man is known as the Hairless Mexican,' he went on.

'Why is he called that?' I asked. It seemed a strange name.

'Because he's hairless and because he's a Mexican,' R. said.

'That seems a very good reason,' I said. 'But I'm still curious. Tell me more about him.'

'When I first met him he was very poor,' said R. 'He had just lost all his land and money in Mexico. He says he was a general in the Mexican Army. If you want to please him, call him General.'

'And what job do you want me to do with him?' I asked.

'The Mexican is going to Italy,' R. said. 'I have a difficult job for him and I want you to go with him. I shall give you some money. When the Mexican has done his job, I want you to give the money to him. I cannot give him the money now because I do not trust him. He is a gambler[1]. If I give him the money now, he will lose it playing cards.'

Now I felt very interested in the Mexican. As a writer I am always interested in different people and their characters. I was sure that the Mexican was a very unusual person.

'Did you come from Switzerland on your own passport?' asked R.

'Yes,' I said.

'You must not use your real name when you travel to Italy with the Mexican,' said R. 'I've got another passport for you. It's a diplomatic passport[2]. The name in the passport is Somerville. You must use this passport when you travel. The Mexican will not know your real name. He will call you Somerville.'

'If the Mexican asks me any questions about myself, what should I tell him?' I asked R.

'Don't worry about that,' said R. 'He won't ask you any questions. The Mexican loves to talk about himself all the time.'

'What is his real name?' I asked.

'His real name is Manuel Carmona,' R. said.

There was silence for a minute or two. I felt that I wanted to ask R. more about the Mexican. Although R. had not told me very much about the man, I was already interested. I wanted to know more about the man before he came into the room.

'There are many things you haven't told me about this man,' I said to R. 'I don't think you trust him, do you?'

R. smiled.

'Not really,' he said. 'His ideas about right and wrong are different from ours. If he needed money, he would steal it from you. But if you needed money, he would give it to you. If you were in trouble, he would help you. If you made him angry, he would kill you. The Hairless Mexican isn't afraid of killing a man.'

I looked closely at R.'s face. I was beginning to learn something important about the Hairless Mexican.

'What is the job?' I asked him.

'A man called Constantine Andreadi is coming from Constantinople,' said R. 'He will be carrying some very important documents[3]. This man is a spy, working for the enemy. Andreadi will arrive in Italy at Brindisi by boat. Then he will go to the German embassy[4] in Rome to give the documents to the Germans. We must stop him doing this.

4

And we must get the documents at all costs[5]. But we must be careful. Italy is still neutral, like Switzerland. We must take care not to get into trouble with the Italians.'

'I see,' I said. 'We must prevent Andreadi from getting to Rome at all costs.'

'Yes,' said R., 'at all costs.'

He repeated the words slowly and carefully. I realized again that this was a very important job. This job was not like any other I had done before.

'I want you and the Hairless Mexican to go down to Brindisi,' continued R. 'The Mexican needs money because he wants to go back to Mexico. I have American dollars with me and I shall give them to you tonight. You had better carry them with you. You will give the money to the Mexican. But don't give him the money until he has given you the documents that Andreadi is carrying.'

'Does the Mexican understand what he has to do?' I asked.

'He understands perfectly,' replied R.

POINTS FOR UNDERSTANDING

Note: The name of the person who is telling this story is Ashenden. In this story he uses a false name: Somerville. But in the questions we have used his real name: Ashenden.

1. What was Ashenden's normal work?
2. Who was 'R.'?
3. Why was Ashenden to go to Italy with the Mexican?
4. Who was Andreadi?
5. When was Ashenden to give the Mexican the money?

2.   The Hairless Mexican

There was a knock at the door of my hotel room. The door
opened and a man stood before us. I realized at once that this
was the Hairless Mexican. R. and I both stood up.

'I have arrived,' the Mexican said, looking at R. 'Good
evening. I am delighted to see you.'

'Good evening,' R. said to the Mexican. 'I'd like you to
meet Mr Somerville. He is going to Brindisi with you.'

'I am pleased to meet you,' the Mexican said to me. He
shook my hand so strongly that my hand hurt.

'Your hands are as strong as iron, General,' I said. I called
him General because I knew it would please him.

The General looked quickly at his hands. His fingernails
were pointed and coloured bright red, and seemed to shine
like mirrors.

'I had them cut and polished this morning,' said the
General. 'I do not think they were very well done. I like my
nails more brightly polished.'

I began to realize that the Mexican was a very unusual
man. I looked at him more closely.

He was a tall man. He was thin, but seemed very powerful.
He was wearing a smart blue suit with a silk handkerchief in
his top pocket. He had a large face and bright brown eyes. He
did not have any hair but he wore a wig[6] of long, untidy hair.
His yellow skin was smooth and he had no eyebrows. His wig
and smooth face and smart clothes made him look a little
frightening. But when you looked at him, there was
something very interesting about him; you could not take
your eyes off him.

The Mexican sat down and looked at me carefully with his
bright brown eyes.

'Are you in the army?' he asked me.

'No, I'm not,' I replied. 'I'm a writer.'

'I am very pleased to meet you, Mr Somerville,' said the

6

Mexican. 'I can tell you many stories that will interest you. I am sure that we will become good friends. I like you, and that is good because we are going to travel together. If I am with a person I don't like, I become very nervous.'

'Thank you, General,' I said. 'I shall be pleased to hear your stories and I am sure we shall have a pleasant journey.'

'When does Mr Andreadi arrive at Brindisi?' asked the Mexican and turned to R.

'He will arrive on the fifteenth,' said R. 'You had better get to Brindisi before he arrives. Mr Somerville knows very little about the job you are going to do, and I don't want you to tell him anything. But if you need his advice, you can ask for it.'

'I never ask other people for advice,' said the Mexican.

'If you don't do the job successfully, don't cause trouble for Mr Somerville,' R. said to the Mexican. 'If you succeed, you will give Mr Somerville the documents and he will pay you the money. He is not interested in how you get the documents.'

'I understand,' said the Mexican.

'Where is your luggage?' R. asked the Mexican.

'I left it at the station,' the Mexican replied.

'When you are on the train, give it to Mr Somerville,' said R. 'He has a special diplomatic passport. At the frontier⁷ the customs men never look through the luggage of people with diplomatic passports.'

'I have very little luggage, only a few suits. But it would be a good idea if Mr Somerville looked after it,' said the Mexican.

'And what about your luggage?' R. asked me.

'I've only got one bag. It's here in my room,' I said.

'That's good,' said R., looking at us both. 'Your train goes tonight at ten minutes past one.'

'Oh?' I said in surprise. I had not realized that we were going to start so soon.

'I think you had both better get down to Brindisi as soon as possible,' explained R.

R. got up from his chair.

'Are there any more questions you would like to ask me?' he said.

'There were still many things I wanted to know about the job. But I was sure that R. did not want to tell us any more.

'I've told you everything,' he said. 'What are you both going to do until your train leaves?'

'I shall take a walk around Lyons,' said the Mexican. 'I have heard that it is an interesting city, and I have not seen it before.'

The Mexican got up, went to the door and turned round.

'Goodnight,' he said to R., 'and pleasant dreams. I do not expect that we shall meet again very soon.'

'I want you to succeed in this job,' R. said to him. 'But if you fail to get the documents you must not cause any trouble for Mr Somerville.'

'You can trust me,' said the Mexican.

He turned to me. 'Goodbye, Mr Somerville,' he said. 'I will meet you again at the station.'

When the Mexican had left the room, R. looked at me with a smile. 'So what do you think of him?' he asked.

'He seems strange and very vain[8],' I said. 'Are you sure you can trust him?'

'I'm not sure,' answered R. 'But we have to take a chance. I believe he will do the job successfully.'

POINTS FOR UNDERSTANDING

1. When were Ashenden and the Mexican going to leave for Brindisi?
2. R. asked Ashenden what he thought of the Mexican. What was Ashenden's reply?
3. Did R. trust the Mexican?

3. The Journey Begins

When I arrived at the station, I went to the waiting-room and sat down in a comfortable seat. I took out a book and began to read. Soon it was time for the train to arrive in the station. I began to feel anxious because the Hairless Mexican had not come. So I went out on to the platform to look for him.

The train for Rome arrived. But I could not see the Hairless Mexican anywhere. I became more and more worried. I walked quickly up and down the platform and looked in all the waiting-rooms, but I could not find him.

What could I do? I decided to get on the train, and I found two seats for us. I stood at the door and looked up and down the platform and looked up at the clock. It was useless for me to travel alone.

I felt very angry with the Mexican and decided to speak to him angrily when he came. There were three minutes to go, then two minutes, then one. It was late at night and the platform was empty because everyone had got on the train.

Then I saw the Hairless Mexican. Behind him were two porters with his luggage, and another man wearing a uniform. They all walked slowly to the train. They did not seem to be in a hurry. Then the Mexican saw me and waved to me.

'Hello,' he said. 'I wondered what had happened to you.'

'Hurry up!' I said impatiently. 'If you don't hurry we shall miss the train.'

'I never miss a train,' said the Mexican. 'Have you got good seats?' He introduced the man in uniform. 'This is the stationmaster[9].'

I nodded at the man in uniform.

The Mexican looked at the seats I had found.

'But this is an ordinary compartment,' the Mexican said in surprise. 'I'm afraid I cannot travel in here.' He turned and spoke to the stationmaster. 'You must find us a better compartment.'

'Certainly, General,' said the stationmaster, 'I will give you the best compartment we have on the train, with beds.'

The stationmaster led us along the train and put us in an empty compartment with two beds. The Mexican looked satisfied.

'That is much better,' said the Mexican. 'I am very grateful to you.' He held out his hand to shake hands with the stationmaster. 'I shall not forget you. I shall tell the Minister how politely you have treated me.'

'That is very kind of you, General,' said the stationmaster. 'I shall be most grateful.'

A whistle blew and the train started to move out of the station.

'This is better than an ordinary compartment, Mr Somerville,' said the Mexican. 'It is always best to travel comfortably.'

I was still angry.

'Why were you so late?' I asked. 'You nearly missed the train. If you had missed the train, all our plans would have been destroyed.'

'There was never any danger that I would miss the train,' replied the Mexican. 'When I arrived, I told the stationmaster that I was General Carmona, the Commander of the Mexican Army. I said that I had to stop in Lyons for a few hours because I had an important meeting with a French Minister. I asked the stationmaster to make the train wait if I was late. I told him that my government would be very grateful and would reward him.'

I did not feel angry any more. I was secretly very amused at the story he had told the stationmaster. I felt sure that the Mexican would be good company for the journey to Rome. I was certain that he knew more interesting stories to tell.

The Mexican took off his boots and lay down on his bed. He lit a cigarette and smoked it.

'Now we must sleep,' he said. 'Goodnight.'

A few minutes later, I heard the Mexican breathing

steadily, and I realized that he was asleep. Soon I myself fell asleep.

After some time I awoke. I saw that the Mexican was still asleep and lay quite still. He had taken off his fur coat and had it over him like a blanket. He still wore his wig.

Suddenly the train slowed down, and stopped with a loud noise from the brakes. Immediately, before I realized that anything had happened, the Mexican jumped up.

'What is it?' he cried.

'Nothing,' I said. 'The train has just stopped, that's all.'

The Mexican sat down on his bed. I turned on the light.

'You awake quickly, although you're such a heavy sleeper,' I said.

'You have to be able to wake quickly in my job,' answered the Mexican.

I would have liked to ask him what his job was. Perhaps it was murder or commanding armies? But I did not ask him and I remained silent. The general opened his bag and took out a bottle of brandy.

'Would you like some brandy?' he asked me. 'It is very good for you when you wake suddenly in the night.'

I refused. The Mexican put the bottle to his lips and poured some of the brandy down his throat. Then he smiled with pleasure and lit a cigarette.

POINTS FOR UNDERSTANDING

1. Why had the stationmaster helped the Mexican so much?
2. What do you think the Mexican meant by 'in my job'?

4. The Following Morning

The train started once more and soon I was asleep again. When I awoke, it was morning. I turned around in my bed and saw that the Mexican was awake too. The floor by his side was covered with cigarette ends and the air was thick and grey with smoke. The window was closed. The Mexican did not want the window open because he thought the night air was dangerous.

'I didn't get up, because I was afraid of waking you,' he said. 'Will you wash first or shall I?'

'I am in no hurry,' I said. 'You can wash first.'

'I have often travelled by train, and I am used to washing quickly,' said the Mexican. 'It will not take me long. Do you clean your teeth every day?'

'Yes,' I said.

'So do I,' said the Mexican. 'It is a habit I learned in New York. I always think that a man should take care of his teeth.'

There was a washbasin in the compartment and the General cleaned his teeth. Then he got a bottle of scented water[10] from his bag and rubbed it over his face and hands. He took a comb from his bag and arranged his wig. He took the bottle of scented water and covered his shirt and coat and handkerchief with scent. The Mexican seemed to be very pleased and satisfied when he had finished.

'Now I am ready,' he said. 'I will leave my things for you and you can use my scent if you want.'

'Thank you very much, but I will not use your scent,' I said. 'All I want is soap and water.'

'Water?' exclaimed the Mexican in surprise. 'I never use water. It is terribly bad for the skin.'

I went to the washbasin and washed with soap and water. Then I got out my razor and shaving things. I shaved and then I felt much better.

The train was near the frontier. I remembered how the General had woken up in the night when the train stopped and had put his hand to his side. I realized that he was probably carrying a gun.

'If you're carrying a gun with you, I think you had better give it to me,' I said. 'I have a diplomatic passport, so they will not search me at the frontier. But they may search you, and we don't want any trouble.'

'It isn't really a weapon, it's more like a little toy,' said the Mexican.

He took a very large gun out of his pocket.

'I do not like to be without it even for an hour,' he continued. 'I do not feel completely dressed without my gun. But you are quite right. We don't want any trouble at the frontier. I will give you my knife as well. I would always rather use a knife than a gun. A knife is a better weapon.'

The Mexican opened his coat and quickly took a knife from his belt. He opened the knife and I looked at it. The knife had a long blade and I knew it was very dangerous. The Mexican looked at me with a smile on his large, ugly, hairless face. I put his knife in my pocket with the gun.

'Have you anything else?' I asked.

'My hands,' said the Mexican proudly, 'but the customs men will not ask about them.'

I remembered how I had shaken hands with the General earlier, and how strong those hands were. I looked at his hands again. They were large and long and smooth. There was not a hair on them. They had red, pointed nails. They looked very frightening.

When our train reached the frontier we got out. We went separately to the office of the customs men. After we had passed through the customs, we returned to our carriage. I handed back the gun and the knife to the Mexican.

'Now I feel more comfortable,' he said, leaning back in his seat. 'I will now tell you a story.'

POINTS FOR UNDERSTANDING

1. What was unusual about the Mexican's hands?
2. What were the Mexican's three weapons?

5. The Death of the Dark Women

The Mexican began to tell me his story. The story was about a girl he had once loved.

'I saw her first in a house in Mexico City,' he began. 'She was going down the stairs as I went up. She was not very beautiful. I had known a hundred women who were more beautiful. But there was something about her that interested me.

15

'An old woman looked after the house where the girl lived. One day I asked the old woman to send the girl to me.

'The old woman said that the girl did not live in the house, but only came from time to time. I told the woman to have the girl there the next evening and to keep her until I came.

'But the next evening I arrived late. The old woman told me that the girl never waited for any man. She had gone. I laughed and gave the old woman some money for the girl. I promised that the next day I would not be late.

'The next day I was not late. But when I arrived, the old woman gave me back my money and said the girl did not like me. I laughed. I took off the diamond ring I was wearing. I told the woman to give it to the girl. Perhaps now she would change her mind[11].

'In the morning the old woman brought me something from the girl in return for my ring. It was a red flower. I did not know whether to be amused or angry.

'But I am always very generous with money. Money is for spending on pretty women. I offered to give the girl a thousand dollars if she would have dinner with me that night. The old woman told this to the girl and the girl agreed to come.

'She came to dinner at my house. I said to you that she was not very beautiful, but I am wrong. She was the most beautiful person I had ever met. I felt that I was madly in love with her.

'You may say I was a fool, but I was the happiest man alive. For seven days I paid a thousand silver dollars for her to eat with me every evening. Every evening I waited for her very nervously. I have never loved anyone else so much before or since. I could think of nothing else.

'I must tell you that when I met her I was a very busy man. I had joined with several other people. We had decided that the country was being badly ruled and that too many people in the country were poor and hungry. We formed a group. We wanted to change the way that our country was ruled. We had money and men. Our plans were ready and I had many things to do. I had to go to meetings, give orders and make everything ready. But I was so in love with this girl that I could do nothing.

'One evening after dinner, the girl lay in my arms. I began to tell her about our plans and about the other people in our group.

'As I told her these things, I felt her body become stiff. She was listening carefully to what I was saying. I suddenly did not trust her.

'I made no sign to the girl that I had noticed anything. She moved closer to me. She said to me that these things frightened her. She asked me if a certain man was in the group. I answered her because I wanted to be certain that she was really interested.

'Very cleverly she persuaded me to give every detail of our plans. Now I was certain that she was a spy. She was one of the President's spies and she had been sent to learn all the secrets and plans of our group. Now she had learned all our secrets. The lives of all of us were in danger. I knew that if she left the room where we were, then I and all the other men would be dead in twenty-four hours.

'And I loved her, I loved her. I cannot describe my feelings. Love like that is no pleasure; it is pain, pain. I knew that she must not leave the room alive. I knew that I had to act quickly. If I waited, I would not have the courage to kill her.

'She said that she would sleep, and soon she was asleep. She was a spy. I had to kill her. But I waited for her to go to sleep before I killed her because I loved her. I did not want her to feel any pain. It is strange that although she was a spy, I was not angry with her.

'I moved my arm and got out my knife. But she was so beautiful that I could not watch what I was doing. I turned my face away and pulled my knife with all my strength across her lovely throat. She did not wake up.'

When the Mexican had told his story, he leaned back in his chair. He made himself a cigarette and lit it. In a moment he seemed much calmer. He seemed to have forgotten about the woman he had loved and killed.

The train arrived in the station at Rome. The station was full of trains, noise and people. A porter came up to us and the Mexican told him to carry our luggage to the Brindisi train.

There were not many people on the Brindisi train, and we found an empty compartment. The Mexican got out a pack of cards and started to play. For some reason I was not able to win a single game, although I sometimes had very good cards. I wondered how the Mexican managed to win. Perhaps he had cheated, but I did not think so. I smiled.

'I am glad to see you smile,' said the Mexican. 'That is very good, because if you can smile when you lose, you will succeed in life. When I am back in Mexico and I have my lands again, you must come and stay with me. I will look after you very well.'

He began to talk about Mexico. He told me about the land which he had owned but which had been taken away from him. I did not know if he was telling the truth or not, but I enjoyed listening to him.

'I lost everything that I owned,' said the Mexican. 'In Paris I had to give Spanish lessons in order to get money to live. I had been very rich in Mexico and I was forced to live like a beggar in Paris. But a man must have patience. His troubles cannot last for ever.'

The train was now nearly at Brindisi. It might be dangerous if people saw us together, and so we decided to stay in separate hotels. The Mexican would come to my hotel only if he had some important news to tell me. If we saw each other by accident in the street, we would not give any sign that we recognized each other.

The train arrived at Brindisi. The Mexican got out first. He was going straight to his hotel. I waited in the station for a few minutes. I pretended to be interested in the newspapers on sale. Finally I bought one and walked out of the station with the paper in one hand and my bag in the other.

I walked to the Hotel Belfast, which was very close to the station. I booked a room. It was late evening now, so I had a quick dinner and then went to bed. I was very tired after a full day travelling with the Mexican.

POINTS FOR UNDERSTANDING

1. Why did the Mexican kill the girl he loved?
2. What does the Mexican's story tell you about the kind of man that he was?
3. Why did Ashenden not want to be seen with the Mexican in Brindisi?

6. Brindisi

The next day I woke up late. I had nothing to do that day. Andreadi's ship was not arriving until the next day. The Mexican would not have any news to bring me now, so I had plenty of time to look around the town.

I had arranged with R. that he would send any orders to the British Consulate[12] in Brindisi. So I went to the Consulate to see if any orders had arrived for me. At the Consulate they told me that everything was all right. They knew who I was and why I had come.

I spent the rest of the day looking around the town. It was May, late spring, and the sun was hot. I walked around all day, looking at museums, churches and the sea.

The next day was the fifteenth of May. This was the day that Andreadi was due to arrive in Brindisi. I decided to stay in my room in the morning for two reasons. Firstly, so that the Mexican could find me easily. Secondly to rest as much as possible, because I might not get much sleep for the next few days.

I was lying on my bed reading a book when the door of my room was quickly opened. A man I did not recognize stood before me.

'What do you want?' I shouted in surprise and fear.

'It's all right. Don't you know me?' said the man.

'Good Lord, it's the Mexican!' I said. 'I didn't recognize you.'

The Mexican had changed his wig. He was now wearing a black wig with short hair. It made him look very different, although his appearance was still very strange. He was also wearing an untidy old grey suit.

'I can only stay here for a minute,' said the Mexican. 'I've found Andreadi. He is in a barber's shop at this minute and he's getting shaved.'

'How did you find him?' I asked.

'That wasn't difficult,' the Mexican replied. 'He was the only Greek person on the ship. I went on to the ship when it arrived. I said I was looking for a Greek friend who was on the ship. I said my friend's name was Diogenidis. Of course nobody had heard of him. I pretended to be very surprised that my friend was not on the ship.

'In this way I started a conversation with Andreadi. Andreadi is travelling under a false name. It it not his real name. He calls himself Lombardos. I followed him when he got off the ship. Do you know the first thing he did? He went into a barber's shop and he had his beard shaved. What do you think of that?'

'Nothing,' I said. 'Lots of people have their beards shaved.'

'That is not what I think,' said the Mexican. 'Andreadi wanted to change his appearance.'

'You have changed your appearance too,' I said.

'Ah, yes,' he said. 'This is a wig I'm wearing. It makes me look different, doesn't it?'

'I didn't recognize you when you came in,' I said.

'One has to be careful,' replied the Mexican. 'But I have more to tell you about Andreadi. He and I are now very close friends. You see, he cannot speak Italian. I helped him and he was grateful. I found him a room here in the Hotel Belfast. He says he is going to Rome tomorrow, but I shall watch him and follow him all the time. I do not want him to escape from me. He says that he wants to see the town now, and I have said that I will show him around.'

'But he does not talk much,' the Mexican went on. 'I tried to get him to talk. He listened to what I said and I saw that he was interested. But he didn't tell me anything about himself. He is carrying the documents on him. They are hidden in his clothes somewhere.'

'How do you know?' I asked.

'He is not worried about his bag, so the documents cannot be in there,' said the Mexican. 'But he puts his hands on his stomach from time to time. The documents must be in a belt or inside his coat.'

'But why did you bring him to stay in this hotel?' I asked.

'I thought it would be easier for us,' he said. 'We may want to search his luggage. And if we find the documents, you can have them immediately. But I must go now. I promised to meet him outside the barber's in fifteen minutes.'

'All right,' I said.

'Where shall I find you tonight if I want you?' asked the Mexican.

'I shall spend the evening in my room,' I said.

'Very well,' he said. 'Will you please look in the passage before I leave. I don't want to meet anybody.'

I opened the door and looked out. There was no one there.

'It's all right,' I said. 'There's nobody about.'

The Hairless Mexican walked out and I closed the door.

A few minutes after the Mexican had left, I went out.

It seemed that the Mexican had found the spy, called Andreadi. I wondered if the Mexican would kill Andreadi to get the secret documents.

Outside the sun was shining brightly. The streets were full of cheerful, lively people as before. But I did not feel happy. I went out and went again to the Consulate to ask if there was a telegram for me. There wasn't. Then I went to the station and asked what time the trains went to Rome. I learned that there was a train at five o'clock in the morning.

I felt bored now with Brindisi. The hot, bright streets tired my eyes, and I did not like the dust and the noise. It was now lunch-time, but I did not feel hungry. I went to a cafe and had a drink. In the afternoon I went to a cinema. Then I went back to my hotel.

I told the owner of the hotel that I would be leaving very early in the morning and so I would pay my bill now. I went up to my room and got my luggage ready. I took my bag to the station and left it there, and then went back to the hotel. All I had with me now in the hotel was a small case. In this case were my code book and one or two other books. I sat down to wait for the Hairless Mexican.

I felt very nervous. I began to read one of the books, but it was not very interesting and I started to read another. But I could not read the book carefully. I was thinking about the Mexican and wondering if he had got the documents yet.

I looked at my watch. It was still very early. I picked up my book again. I said to myself that I would read thirty pages before I looked at my watch again. I read several pages but I could not read properly or remember what I was reading.

I looked at the time again. It was only half past ten. I wondered where the Hairless Mexican was now and what he was doing. I was afraid that he would make a mistake. I got up and shut the window and closed the curtains. I smoked one cigarette after the other. I looked at my watch and it was a quarter past eleven.

It was a warm night but my hands and feet were cold. My mind began to think about murder. I did not want to think about this subject, but I was a writer and had a strong imagination. Now I could not control this imagination. I asked myself how one would murder someone in Brindisi. I began to think of the different places and different ways one could murder someone.

I looked at my watch again. I now felt very tired with all the waiting. I did not even try to read any more. I sat without thinking of anything and without doing anything.

Then the door opened quietly and I jumped up. I felt frightened. The Hairless Mexican stood before me.

POINTS FOR UNDERSTANDING
1. Why did the Mexican think that Lombardos was Andreadi?
2. Why did the Mexican think that the documents must be in Lombardos' belt or in his coat?
3. Why did Ashenden not enjoy reading his book?
4. Why did Ashenden keep thinking about murder?

7. The Search for the Papers

'Did I frighten you?' asked the Mexican and smiled.

'Yes,' I said. 'Did anyone see you come in?'

'I was let in by the night porter. He was asleep when I rang the bell. He didn't look at me carefully when he opened the door. I'm sorry I'm so late, but I had to change.'

The Hairless Mexican was wearing again the clothes he had worn on the train, and his fair wig. He looked very different again. His eyes were shining and he seemed very happy. He looked at me closely.

'How white you are, my friend!' he said. 'Surely you are not nervous?'

'Have you got the documents?' I asked.

'No,' said the Mexican. 'Andreadi wasn't carrying the documents in his clothes. This is all he was carrying.'

The Mexican put down a thick pocket-book and a passport.

'I don't want them,' I said quickly. 'You can keep them.'

The Hairless Mexican put the things back in his pocket.

'What was in his belt?' I asked. 'You said Andreadi kept putting his hands on his stomach.'

'There was only money in his belt,' the Mexican answered. 'I've looked through the pocket book. It contains nothing but private letters and some photographs. He must have locked the documents in his bag before he came out with me this evening.'

'Damn[13]!' I said. I felt very angry at this news.

'It doesn't matter,' said the Mexican. 'I've got the key of his room. We can go and look through all his luggage.'

I felt sick and afraid. The Mexican smiled at me.

'There is no danger,' he said, as if he was talking to a small boy. 'But if you don't feel happy, I'll go alone.'

'No, I'll come with you,' I said.

'There's no-one awake in the hotel, and Mr Andreadi won't be there. Take off your shoes if you like,' said the Mexican.

I did not answer. I noticed that my hands were shaking slightly and this made me angry. Then I took off my shoes and the Mexican did the same.

'You had better go first,' said the Mexican. 'Turn to the left and go straight along the passage. Andreadi's room is number thirty-eight.'

I opened the door and stepped out. The passage was not well lit. I was angry because I was feeling nervous, and I knew that the Mexican was not nervous at all.

We reached the door of room number thirty-eight. The Mexican turned the key in the lock and went in. He switched on the light. I followed him and closed the door.

'Now we are all right,' said the Mexican. 'We need not hurry.'

He took some keys out of his pocket and tried to open Andreadi's suitcase. With the third key he succeeded in opening it. The suitcase was filled with clothes. He took the clothes out of the suitcase and felt them carefully. There were no papers of any sort in the case. Then the Mexican took out his knife and cut the lining of the suitcase. There were no documents hidden in the lining.

'The documents are not here,' said the Mexican angrily. 'They must be hidden in the room.'

'Are you sure he didn't give the documents to somebody?' I asked.

'That is not possible,' said the Mexican. 'I was watching Andreadi all the time, except when he was getting shaved,' the Mexican answered.

He opened the drawers and the cupboard. He looked under the bed, in the bed, and under the mattress. He looked around the floor, which had no carpet. His eyes looked up and down the room, trying to discover a hiding-place and I felt that nothing escaped his eyes.

'Perhaps Andreadi left the documents downstairs with the porter,' I said.

'But he would not dare leave them with the porter,' said the Mexican. 'The papers are not here either. I can't understand it.'

The Mexican looked around the room. He did not know what to do next. He was wondering what had happened to the documents.

I was beginning to feel really frightened now.

'Let's get out of here,' I said.

'In a minute,' the Mexican said.

He went down on his knees, folded the clothes quickly and neatly and packed them up again. He locked the case and stood up. Then he put out the light, and slowly opened the door and looked out. He made a sign to me and we went out into the passage. He stopped and locked the door, and put the key in his pocket. We went back to my room. When we were inside, I locked the door.

The Mexican looked at me and saw that I was nervous and afraid.

'There wasn't really the smallest danger,' said the Mexican. 'But what are we to do now? Your boss[14] will be angry that the documents haven't been found.'

'I'm going to Rome on the five o'clock train,' I said. 'I shall ask for orders when I get there.'

'Very well, I will come with you,' said the Mexican.

'Wouldn't it be better if you left Italy as soon as possible?' I asked. 'There's a boat tomorrow that goes to Spain. Why don't you travel on it? If necessary I can then come and see you in Spain.'

'I see that you want to say goodbye,' said the Mexican with a smile. 'Very well. I will go to Spain.'

I looked at my watch. It was a little after two o'clock. I had nearly three hours to wait until my train left for Rome. The Mexican made himself a cigarette. Then he turned again to me.

'Shall we have a little supper?' he suggested. 'I'm very hungry.'

Although I had not eaten all day, I did not feel very hungry. I did not want to go out with the Hairless Mexican, but I did not want to stay by myself in the hotel, either.

'It is very late,' I said. 'Where can we find a place open at such an hour?'

'Come with me. I'll find you a place,' said the Mexican.

I put on my hat and picked up my case. We left the room and went downstairs.

POINTS FOR UNDERSTANDING

1. What did the Mexican mean by the words 'Mr Andreadi won't be there?'
2. How had the Mexican failed in his job?
3. Where was Ashenden going and where was the Mexican going?

8. The Telegram

In the hall of the hotel the porter was asleep on a mattress on the floor. We walked softly past him in order not to wake him. I noticed a letter addressed to me on the desk. I picked it up carefully, and opened it when we were just outside the door.

The letter was from the Consulate. It said: 'The enclosed telegram arrived last night and in case it is important I am sending it to you immediately.' I opened the telegram and saw that it was in code. We were both in a hurry to go and eat, so I decided to read the telegram later.

I folded it up and put it in my wallet. I followed the Hairless Mexican who walked quickly through the streets. At last we came to a tavern and went in.

The tavern was a long, unpleasant, dirty room. At one end of it a young man with an old man's face sat at a piano. There were tables and benches along the walls. A number of young men and women were sitting at the tables. They were drinking beer and wine. The women looked old and very ugly.

I did not like the tavern. I wanted to leave. But the Mexican would not let me.

'It is a good place, you will see,' he said to me. 'Here you can eat well and cheaply, and you can dance, too.'

I looked at the women. I did not agree with the Mexican, and still wanted to leave.

'At this time of night, this is the only place where we can get a meal,' he said.

There was nothing else I could do. We sat down at a table. Everybody was staring at us. I felt very embarrassed[15] and tried not to look at the other people as they stared. A waiter came and the Mexican ordered two plates of macaroni and a bottle of wine. Then the Mexican looked around at the women who were sitting at the other tables.

28

The pianist started to play, and several people got up and began to dance.

'Do you dance?' the Mexican asked me. He did not wait for me to answer, but went on immediately. 'I'm going to ask one of these girls to get up and dance with me.'

He got up and went to a girl sitting alone at one of the tables. She was not very pretty, but the Mexican seemed happy and danced well. He began to talk to the woman and she seemed interested in what he was saying.

When the dance finished, the Mexican took her back to her table. He came back to our table.

'What do you think of my girl?' he asked, but again he did not wait for me to reply.

'Dancing is good for you,' he continued. 'Why don't you ask one of the girls to dance with you? This is a nice place, isn't it? I can always find a nice place like this in any town.'

The pianist started to play again and the Mexican again got up to dance.

Then the waiter brought two big plates of macaroni to our table. When the Mexican saw the macaroni, he stopped dancing immediately. He left the woman without taking her back to her table, and hurried to our table.

We both began to eat. The Mexican ate greedily. He was enjoying eating as much as he had enjoyed dancing.

'Well, my friend, are you feeling better?' he asked me with a smile.

As he said this, he leaned forward to touch me on the arm.

'What's that?' I shouted in sudden surprise.

I pointed to the end of the Mexican's shirt-sleeve.

'What's that red stain on your cuff?'

The Hairless Mexican looked at the end of his sleeve.

'That?' asked the Mexican. 'That is nothing. It's only blood. I had a little accident and I cut myself.'

I was silent. Many thoughts now came into my mind. I remembered what R. had said about the Mexican. I knew that

the Mexican was not afraid of killing a man. The Mexican had
killed a man that evening. And here he was, talking and
laughing as if nothing had happened.

But I did not get angry. This was war and we had each
been given a job to do. Soon I would have to speak to the
Mexican, and I did not want to. I would have to tell him that I
could not give him the money because he had not given me
any documents. I wondered what he would say. But I would
have to speak to him soon; I had to catch a train. I looked at
the clock.

The Mexican saw me look at the clock.

'I understand you are in a hurry to catch your train,' he
said. 'Let me have one more dance and then we will go.'

He got up and started dancing with the same woman. I
watched him. His movements reminded me of a lion or a
tiger. He danced beautifully, but I thought too how

31

dangerous he could be. I wished I could get up and leave him, but we had to have our conversation.

At last the music stopped and he came back. I paid the bill and we left. It was a warm night, so we walked to the station. There were stars in the sky and the air was still. There was complete silence all round.

We entered the station, which was almost empty. There were only one or two porters and two soldiers. They were all standing quite still. The station seemed to be very quiet at this time of morning. The waiting-room was empty and we went in.

Then I remembered the telegram which I had not read.

'I still have an hour before my train goes,' I said. 'I'll just see what this telegram says.'

I took the telegram out of my wallet and got the book with the code out of my case. I started working to decode the message.

The Hairless Mexican sat in the corner. He made himself cigarettes and smoked them. He sat there happily, and took no notice of what I was doing. I looked up at him. He looked like a man who has done a good piece of work and is now resting, proud of what he has done.

I worked at the message. Whenever I had to decode a message like this I always wrote down the letters and the words without thinking of their meaning. I did not look at the meaning until I had finished the message. Then I read it.

It said:

'Constantine Andreadi is ill at Athens. He will be unable to sail to Brindisi. You should return to Geneva.'

As first I could not understand. I read the message again. I shook with surprise and shock. Then I could not remain silent any longer. I turned to the Mexican.

'You fool,' I shouted, 'you've killed the wrong man!'

POINTS FOR UNDERSTANDING

1. Why did Ashenden not read the telegram immediately?
2. What did Ashenden notice on the Mexican's sleeve?
3. Why had they found no documents in the dead man's room earlier that afternoon?

The Traitor

1. Another Job

After my adventure in Italy with the Hairless Mexican, I went back to Switzerland, to the city of Geneva. I started to work again on the book that I was writing.

I had been back for three months, and it was now summer. One day I had a letter from my boss, R. It was in code. I got out my code book and worked out what the letter said. The letter said I must go to a certain park in Geneva at two o'clock the next afternoon and I would meet R. there. R. had another job for me. He would tell me all about it when we met.

We met the next afternoon in the park.

'Ashenden,' said R., 'I want you to go to a town called Lucerne. There is an Englishman living in a hotel there. His name is Grantley Caypor. His wife is German. Because she is a German, they cannot live in England. Caypor and his wife have to live in Switzerland because it is a neutral country.'

'Why are you interested in this man?' I asked.

'Because he is a traitor[16],' R. said.

R. told me everything he knew about this man. Caypor was forty-two, and had been married for eleven years. They had no children. Caypor had had several different jobs in his life, and had lived in different countries. Twice he had been put in prison for stealing small amounts of money.

'So you see,' said R., 'he is not a very honest man. When he came here to Switzerland at the beginning of the war, he started to work as a spy for the enemy.'

'But if you know that he is a spy, why haven't you done anything about it?' I asked.

'We know all the information which he gives to the enemy

because our spies open his letters,' said R. 'The letters are in code, but we have learned the code so we can read the letters. The information he gives the enemy is not important, so it doesn't matter if the enemy learn it. Sometimes we have been able to give him false information, which confuses[17] the enemy.'

'Then why do you want me to do something about him now?' I asked.

'Caypor did a very nasty thing last month,' said R. 'He found out that a Swiss man was working as a spy for us. This spy went into Germany to get more information for us. Caypor told the Germans that the man was a spy, and they shot him.'

'So what do you want me to do?' I asked.

'I have an idea,' said R. 'Caypor has betrayed his country in return for money. If we offered him more money, perhaps he would spy for us against the Germans. This would be very useful for us, because we know that the Germans trust Caypor already. He could give us very valuable information.'

R. was silent for a moment. I waited. I knew that in a minute he would continue. He would tell me exactly what he wanted me to do.

'But we would like to know more about Caypor,' said R. 'What kind of a man is he? You could find this out for us. I want you to go to Lucerne and get to know him. If you think that he would work for the British, then you could suggest this idea to him. But you would have to do it very carefully. He must not realize that you are a spy.'

'And if I think that he would not work for the British?' I asked. 'What would happen then?'

'Then you will just watch him,' continued R. 'You will tell us where he goes and the people he meets. But I must tell you one more thing. We have learned that the Germans are not satisfied with Caypor. The Germans are paying him a lot of money but he is not giving them enough information.'

'They will persuade him that he should do more for them,'
went on R. 'Perhaps they will suggest that he should go to
England and spy for them. Then your job is to help Caypor so
that he can get to England. But you must be very careful so
that he isn't suspicious[18] of you.'

'And if he gets to England, what will happen to him then?'
I asked.

'We shall shoot him, like they shot our man,' R. said simply
and calmly.

'You are asking me to do a difficult job,' I said. 'From what
you have said, Caypor seems very clever.'

'You must be cleverer than Caypor,' said R. 'That is why
we pay you!'

POINTS FOR UNDERSTANDING

Note: The name of the person who is telling this story is again
    Ashenden. In this story he again uses a false name: Somerville.
    But in the questions we have used his real name: Ashenden.

1. Why could the Caypors not live in England?
2. Where were they living?
3. What was Caypor's job?
4. What was the very nasty thing that Caypor had done?
5. What were the two things that Ashenden was to try to persuade
   Caypor to do?

2. I Go to Lucerne

I left R. in the park and went back to where I was living. I
started to pack my bags because I was going to Lucerne the
next day. I had a false passport with me, in the name of
Somerville. While I was doing this job for R., I would pretend
that my name was Somerville.

I would go to the hotel where Caypor was staying in

Lucerne. If Caypor asked me questions about myself, I would tell him that I had been very ill in England recently. I would tell him that I had come to Switzerland to get better. Everybody knows that mountain air is very good for someone who is not well. So Caypor would certainly believe me. My skin was always rather pale. This pale skin made me look slightly ill, even when I was not.

If Caypor asked me, I would also tell him that in England I worked for a government department[19]. I would let him think that I knew some government secrets. I would also give him some false information which he could pass on to the enemy. In this way he would slowly begin to trust me. Perhaps this would make it easy for me to persuade him to go to England.

The next day I got up early to catch the train to Lucerne. It was a fine summer day, and there was not a cloud in the sky.

I arrived in Lucerne early in the afternoon, and went to the hotel where Caypor was staying. I booked a room and put my things in it. Then, because it was such a fine day, I went out for a walk beside the lake.

I was not in a hurry to meet Caypor. I thought it would seem much more natural if I showed no interest in him. I would wait until he came to me and started to talk. If I went up to him and started telling him about myself, he would be suspicious. So I just pretended that I was recovering from a serious illness. I decided to spend my days walking around Lucerne, enjoying myself.

It was a beautiful afternoon. I had been to Lucerne five years earlier. But that was before the war, and there had been crowds of people in the streets and cafes beside the lake. Now there was almost nobody. Most of the hotels were closed and the streets were empty. The boats were not used because there were no visitors who wanted to go on the lake. Before the war there were people from all over Europe here. Now there was nobody except the Swiss and a very few foreigners.

I like being on my own, so I sat down on a seat by the

water. I looked out at the blue water of the lake and the mountains on the other side of the lake. It was very peaceful. It was difficult to believe that a war was going on in the rest of Europe.

I got up and walked slowly back to the hotel. It was a small, clean hotel, and my bedroom had a nice view of the town and the lake. I washed and went down to the small dining-room. I sat down at a table and the landlady came over to me. I ordered a bottle of beer. The landlady brought it.

The landlady was curious to know about me. She asked me why I had come to stay. She asked if I was ill because my skin looked so pale. I told her that I had been very ill recently and had come here to get better.

The landlady asked me what my job was. I told her that I worked in a government department. I said that now that I was here, I wanted to practise speaking German. I had learnt German many years before, and had forgotten a lot.

The landlady was a friendly, talkative Swiss woman. I felt sure that she would tell Caypor everything I told her. Since she seemed to have plenty of time, I decided to ask the landlady a few questions.

I asked her if the hotel was always so empty in August.

'Oh no,' she replied. 'The hotel was always very full in other years. We did not have enough room for everyone who wanted to stay here. But now this terrible war! It has stopped everybody from coming here. Sometimes people come in just for a meal, but we have only two couples[20] staying in the hotel. One is an old Irish couple, and the other couple is an Englishman with a German wife. Because she is German, they have to live in a neutral country.'

I realized that she was talking about the Caypors, but I took care to show no curiosity about them. The landlady was talkative, and had nothing else to do except tell me about the Caypors.

'They are usually in the mountains for most of the day,' she told me. 'Mr Caypor is interested in the plants and flowers.

We have so many interesting flowers in the mountains around here. His wife is very unhappy about the war. But the war cannot last for ever.'

The landlady went into the kitchen to prepare dinner, and I went up to my room.

POINTS FOR UNDERSTANDING

1. What was Somerville's real name?
2. What reason did Ashenden give for coming to Lucerne?
3. What did Ashenden say he was working for in England?
4. Why did Ashenden want Caypor to speak to him first?
5. Why did Ashenden think that Caypor would learn all about him from the landlady?

3. The Caypors

Dinner was at seven o'clock. I went down to the dining-room at a quarter to seven. I went early so that I would be the first in the dining-room. I wanted to watch the other people as they came in.

Two or three men came in separately and sat at separate tables. They looked Swiss and read newspapers while they ate their soup noisily.

Then a tall old man with white hair and a white moustache came in. With him was a little white-haired old lady in black. They certainly were not the Caypors. It was the Irish couple the landlady had spoken about. They sat down and waited in silence for their dinner to be brought to them.

At last the couple arrived that I had been waiting for. I had with me a German book which I pretended to read. I looked up only for a moment as the Caypors came in. I did not want to show too much interest in the Caypors at the beginning.

When I raised my eyes, I saw a middle-aged man with

short hair. He was of medium height, rather fat, with a broad red face. He wore a shirt open at the neck, and a grey suit.

So this was the spy, I thought. This was the man I might have to try to persuade to go to England.

Grantley Caypor and his wife sat down at their table. He began talking loudly to the waitress in German.

I knew enough German to understand what he was saying. He said that they had been out for a very long walk, and had gone up a mountain; he gave the name of the mountain. I did not know the name and it meant nothing to me.

I watched Caypor carefully out of the corner of my eye, while I pretended to read my book. I noticed that he looked very cheerful and friendly.

The waitress went out, and Caypor shouted after her.

'Bring the food quickly,' he said. 'We're very hungry. And bring a bottle of beer. I'm so thirsty after our long walk.'

Caypor began to talk to his wife in English. Everything he said could be heard by the other people in the room. After a moment she said something to him so quietly that I could not hear. Caypor stopped speaking. He looked at me while I pretended to read my book. I was sure that Mrs Caypor had noticed me first. She had told her husband that there was a stranger in the dining-room.

I pretended to be reading still, and turned over the page of the book. Caypor spoke to his wife, but very quietly. The waitress brought their food. Caypor asked her a question, and I knew that he must be asking who I was. I could not hear what the waitress said to him.

One or two people finished their dinner and went out. The Irish couple got up and left, and I went out a little later. In the hall outside the dining-room, I saw a small dog tied to the leg of a table. I like animals, and I put my hand down to pat it.

The landlady was standing close by. I looked up at her.

'Whose is this dog?' I asked. 'He's a fine dog.'

'He belongs to Mr Caypor,' said the landlady. 'His name is Fritzi. Mr Caypor is very proud of his dog.'

The dog was friendly, and put his nose in my hand. I left him and went on upstairs to get my hat. I had decided to go for a walk and sit somewhere pleasant to have a cup of coffee.

When I came downstairs with my hat, I saw Caypor at the entrance of the hotel. He was talking with the landlady. When he saw me, he suddenly became silent. I guessed that Caypor had been asking the landlady about me. When I went out of the door, I passed between Caypor and the landlady. Out of the corner of my eye, I saw Caypor give me a suspicious look. His face, which had been so cheerful at dinner, now looked unfriendly.

I walked beside the lake until I found a cafe where I could sit outside. I felt pleased because at last I had seen the man. I had heard so much about him, and soon I would get to know him. He had a dog and that was good. It is easy to talk to an Englishman if he has a dog. It is easy because you can start by talking about his dog, and the man will always answer with pleasure and interest.

I was in no hurry to get to know him, as I have said. I would wait until Caypor spoke to me before I spoke to him. Perhaps it was true that Caypor's boss was not satisfied with his work. Then Caypor would want to speak to me. He thought that I was working for a British government department. Caypor must think that I knew secrets. If he could learn these secrets, he could pass them on to his boss who would then be pleased with him.

POINTS FOR UNDERSTANDING

1. Why did Ashenden not want the Caypors to know that he was interested in them?
2. Did the Caypors notice at dinner that Ashenden had arrived in the hotel?
3. Why was Ashenden pleased that the Caypors had a dog?
4. Why would Caypor be interested in talking to Ashenden?

4. A Conversation with Caypor

It was my second day at the hotel. I was sitting in the sun just outside the door of the hotel. I had eaten a big lunch and I was now drinking a cup of coffee, and feeling very sleepy. Suddenly I felt something small touch my leg. It was Fritzi, the Caypors' dog. He jumped up at me in a friendly way.

'Come here, Fritzi!' shouted Caypor. Then he turned to me. 'I'm so sorry. But he's quite gentle. He won't hurt you.'

'That's all right,' I said. 'But he's an unusual dog, isn't he? You don't often see this type of dog in Switzerland.'

While I spoke, I could see Caypor looking at me carefully. I thought he was trying to understand what kind of person I was. At that moment, the waitress came out to the next table. She picked up some empty cups. Caypor turned to her.

'Could I have a cup of coffee, please?' he asked her. Then he turned back to me. 'You've just arrived, haven't you?'

'Yes, I came yesterday,' I answered.

'Really?' he said. 'I didn't see you in the dining-room last night. Will you be staying here for very long?'

'I don't know,' I said, and this was the truth. 'I've been ill, and I've come here to get better. The doctor said that the mountain air would help me.'

The waitress came with the coffee. She looked at Caypor for a moment, and saw that he was talking to me. She put down the tray with his coffee on my table.

'I'm sorry,' Caypor said immediately. 'I don't know why the waitress put my coffee on your table. I'll take it and drink it inside.'

'No, no, please sit down,' I said.

He thought I was just saying this to be polite. Of course I wanted to be polite, but Caypor did not know that he was beginning to fall into the trap.[21]

'That's very kind of you,' said Caypor. 'By the way, are you English or American?'

45

'English,' I said.

I am really a very shy person. I have often wished that I wasn't shy. I have tried many times to become less shy. But now I thought that my shyness would be useful. If Caypor thought that I was shy, he would feel more relaxed with me. If he saw that I was shy, he would naturally talk more to me. I could learn all about him. He would never think that a shy person like me was leading him into a trap.

I explained slowly about my illness and why I had come to Switzerland. It was the same story as I told the landlady. I was sure that the landlady had already told Caypor my story.

'Lucerne is really the best place for you,' said Caypor. 'It is a place where you can find peace. Here in Lucerne, you can forget that there is a war going on in other countries. That is why I have come here to Lucerne, because it is so peaceful. I'm a journalist.'

I gave a shy smile. 'Oh, really?' I said, pretending to show interest.

'You see,' said Caypor seriously, 'I married a German lady.'

'Yes, I see,' I said. 'So you couldn't stay in England because England is at war with Germany.'

'Yes,' said Caypor. 'I love England. But when the war started, people in England were very unkind to my wife. Everyone thought she was a spy. That was very stupid. She's a housewife. She only cares for our house and me and our child Fritzi.'

Caypor bent down to pat his dog, and gave a little laugh.

'Yes, Fritzi is just like a child to us,' he said.

I smiled politely, but I said nothing. Caypor went on talking.

'When people thought that my wife was a spy, it made things very difficult for me. In my work as a journalist I was working on some secret papers. The people I worked for could not let me continue to work on them because my wife was a German. So I decided to leave England and come to a neutral country until the war finished. And that is why we are here. But my wife and I never discuss the war together.'

'I should like you to meet my wife,' Caypor went on. 'By the way, I don't know if you know my name. I'm Grantley Caypor.'

'My name is Somerville,' I said.

I told him more about myself. I said that in England I worked for a government department. It seemed to me that Caypor's eyes showed special interest when I said that. I also said that I was looking for someone who could give me German conversation lessons, because I wanted to practise my German.

As I said this, I suddenly had an idea. I looked at Caypor and realized that he had the same idea. We had both thought that Mrs Caypor could be my teacher. It would be a good plan for Caypor because he might learn more about me and my work. He would be able to pass more information on to the enemy. It would be a good plan for me because Caypor would fall into the trap. I would learn more about him and his wife. I could then decide whether he could be persuaded to work for us or not.

'I asked our landlady if she could find a teacher for me,' I said after a short silence. 'She said she could probably find me one. I must ask her again, and I'm sure I'll find a teacher.'

'Don't trust the landlady,' said Caypor. 'If she finds a teacher for you, I'm sure the teacher will speak the local dialect[22]. The local dialect is not good for you to learn. I'll ask my wife if she knows anyone. My wife is an educated woman, and you can trust her.'

'That's very kind of you,' I said.

I looked carefully at Caypor. Even when his face was cheerful, I noticed that his eyes looked suspicious. When Caypor smiled and talked he seemed cheerful. But his eyes were always cold.

'I suppose you know a little German?' Caypor asked me with interest.

47

'Yes,' I said. 'I was a student in Germany. I used to speak German very well, but that was a long time ago. I can still read it easily.'

'Oh, yes, I noticed you were reading a German book last night,' said Caypor.

The fool! Caypor was a fool! He had told me just now that he had not seen me in the dining-room last night. That was a mistake. I wondered if Caypor realized his mistake.

Caypor got up.

'Excuse me,' he said, 'my wife will come in a moment. It is time for our walk. We always go for a walk every afternoon in the mountains. The flowers are lovely. You must come with us one day.'

'I am afraid I must wait until I am a little stronger,' I said.

Mrs Caypor came downstairs and her husband joined her. They walked down the road with their dog. Caypor began talking loudly to his wife. I was sure he was telling her about our conversation.

I was still feeling sleepy so I got up and went to my room. In a few minutes I was asleep.

POINTS FOR UNDERSTANDING

1. Why was Ashenden's shyness useful?
2. Why did Ashenden want Mrs Caypor to teach him German?
3. Why did Caypor want his wife to teach Ashenden?
4. What was the mistake that Caypor made?

5. A Lesson with Mrs Caypor

When I woke up, it was already evening. I went down again to the dining-room for dinner. As I went in, I saw the Caypors just getting up from a table. They had just finished their meal. As they came towards me, Caypor spoke to me.

'We would be very pleased if you could join us for coffee outside, after you have finished your meal,' Caypor said to me.

'I certainly will,' I said.

I had a good meal, and then I went out to join them. Caypor got up and introduced me to his wife.

'I'm pleased to meet you,' I said politely.

Mrs Caypor moved her head a little, as if to show that she

had heard me. But she did not say a word, and there was no smile on her face. It was easy to see that she did not like me.

Now I was able to look at her clearly for the first time. She was a woman of about forty years old. She had some spots on her face and she did not look healthy. But I could see that she was not a stupid woman. Caypor had said that she was just a housewife. But I had lived in Germany and I had known many women who looked just like her. Although she probably was a good housewife, I knew that she probably also very intelligent.

She wore a white blouse, a black skirt and heavy boots suitable for walking in the mountains.

Caypor spoke to her in English. He told her in his usual cheerful, smiling way what I had told him about myself. I was sure that he must have told her all this once already. She listened with an unfriendly look on her face.

Caypor turned to me.

'You told me that you spoke German,' he said. His face had a smile, but his eyes moved coldly.

'Yes, I was a student for some time in Germany, at Heidelberg University,' I replied.

'Really?' said Mrs Caypor, in English. She suddenly seemed more interested in me. 'I know Heidelberg well,' she said. 'I was at school there for one year.'

Mrs Caypor spoke very correct English, but she did not speak like an English person. I did not like the way she spoke. I had decided that I would be pleasant to her. I had no reason to be rude. But I could see that she thought she was better than me. She thought that she was superior.

'I have not told you, my dear,' said Caypor. 'Mr Somerville is looking for someone to give him conversation lessons while he is here. I told him that you might suggest a teacher for him.'

'No, I know no one here,' she answered. 'The local dialect here is very bad. If Mr Somerville found a local teacher, it would not help his German at all.'

'Mr Somerville,' said Caypor, 'I suggest you ask my wife to

give you German lessons. She is, if I may say so, an intelligent woman.'

'Oh, Grantley, I haven't the time,' said Mrs Caypor. 'I have my own work to do.'

I saw that they were giving me a chance to accept Caypor's suggestion. I pretended to become shy again, and I turned to Mrs Caypor.

'Of course, it would be wonderful if you could give me lessons,' I said. 'I should be very grateful. I wouldn't want to stop you from doing your work. I am just here to get well. I have nothing at all to do, and I could have the lessons at any time that you wanted.'

I watched them carefully, and I was sure that I saw a look of interest in their eyes as I spoke.

'Of course, it would be only fair that you should pay my wife something for the lessons,' said Caypor.

'You are quite right,' I said. 'Of course, I will pay something for the lessons.'

Caypor turned to his wife.

'What do you say, my dear?' he asked her. 'Surely you can find an hour when you are not busy. The lessons would help Mr Somerville. He would also learn that not all Germans are bad, as people think in England.'

Mrs Caypor thought for a moment. I wondered how we could have an hour's conversation every day. What would we find to talk about? I would find it very difficult to think of anything to talk about with her.

'I shall be very pleased to give Mr Somerville conversation lessons,' she said at last.

It was clear that she was not very happy. She was doing it only because this was a plan which would help her husband.

'Well, Mr Somerville, you are very lucky to have found such a teacher,' said Caypor in a loud voice. 'When will you start? Tomorrow morning at eleven?'

'That will be a good time for me if it is all right for Mrs Caypor,' I said.

'Yes, that is a good time,' Mrs Caypor said. 'I will come to your room and give you your lesson there.'

I got up and said thank you and goodbye to them.

At eleven o'clock the next morning there was a knock at my door. I opened it and Mrs Caypor came in. I was feeling a little afraid. I would have to talk with her for an hour, and I could not think of anything to talk about. I also had to be very careful that she would not suspect me, so I had to watch my words. I knew that she was a very intelligent woman.

She sat down and started immediately to ask me questions about German literature. She corrected my mistakes very carefully. When I had some difficulties with German grammar, she explained things clearly. I could see that she did not enjoy giving me lessons. But I quickly found out that she was a very good teacher. She seemed to love teaching. As our conversation continued, I could see that she was beginning to forget that our two countries, England and Germany, were at war.

Later in the day I met Caypor just outside the hotel.

'Well, Mr Somerville,' he said with a cheerful smile on his face, 'how did your lesson go?'

I told him the truth.

'It was a very good lesson.' I said. 'Your wife is an excellent teacher, and a very interesting person to talk to.'

He laughed.

'I told you so, didn't I?' he said. 'My wife is the cleverest woman I know.'

I felt that when Caypor said this, he was being honest for the first time since I had met him.

We had a lesson every day for the next three days. Mrs Caypor would only talk about music and literature. On the fourth day I asked her something about the war. She stopped me immediately.

'I think that is something we had better not talk about, Mr

Somerville,' she said. I never spoke about the war again.

She continued to work hard at her lessons. She was very unfriendly, but she seemed interested in teaching. I tried various ways to become more friendly with her, but she still did not like me.

Now I had got to know her fairly well, and I realized why she disliked me. She disliked me because I was English. She could not like me because we came from countries at war with each other. But at the same time she knew a lot about literature, painting and music. All this gave me a lot to think about.

POINTS FOR UNDERSTANDING

1. What happened when Ashenden tried to talk to Mrs Caypor about the war?
2. Why did Mrs Caypor dislike Ashenden?

6. I Decide How to Act

I sat in my room looking across the lake. It was a fine morning, and I felt happy after a good breakfast. I was sure that the Caypors did not realize that I was a spy. I had got to know them, and the plan was working well. They believed my story that I was here to recover from an illness. I thought about what I knew of the Caypors.

I could understand Mrs Caypor more easily than her husband. She obviously hated me. Although she was polite to me during the lessons, she hated me so much that sometimes she was rude to me. One day she told me that the English knew nothing about literature. On another day I heard her say 'Stupid man' to herself quietly in German. I was sure that she would be ready to kill me if she ever discovered that I was a British spy.

It was strange then that she could love her husband so much. I noticed how she often held his hand and looked lovingly at him. It seemed that she loved her husband because he admired her. She also liked Caypor's cheerfulness and his jokes. She felt that she protected him like a mother protects a child.

But I reminded myself that Caypor was a spy. Did Mrs Caypor know this? Yes, I was certain that she must have known her husband was a spy.

Mrs Caypor believed that Germany was better than England in every way. It was probably her idea that her husband should spy for the Germans. Caypor would not have become a spy if his wife had not persuaded him. I wondered how she had persuaded him and what she had said to him. I could imagine many things, but I could not know what she said for certain.

I thought about Caypor himself. I remembered everything that R. had told me about his past. He was not a man to admire. But there were many surprising things about him. There was one side of him which was a spy, and which had sent a man to his death. There was another side of him which was cheerful and told jokes and laughed. He was always ready to help people. He was very good to the Irish couple in the hotel, and sometimes brought them little presents and flowers.

Now that I knew Caypor a little, I found him an interesting man. He was far more interesting than anyone I could invent in a story. I wondered again why he had wanted to become a spy. I did not think he had become a spy just for the money. There were other ways of earning money than becoming a spy. He could have earned more money in another, less dangerous job.

I could also see that Caypor was a careful man with money. He did not spend a lot of money and so he did not need a lot of money.

Perhaps he had become a spy because he hated the English. They had put him in prison when he was caught stealing. Perhaps he had not been persuaded by his wife.

Or perhaps he was a spy because he was a dishonest man. He had only been to prison twice, but perhaps he had been dishonest on many other occasions.

It was impossible for me to know any of these things for certain. But thinking about the Caypors helped me to make my ideas clearer. I still did not understand Caypor's character. I did not know why he had chosen to work as a spy. And the two sides to his character? Was he a good man who loved evil, or an evil man who loved good? I did not understand how these two sides could exist in the same man.

Only one thing was clear to me. Grantley Caypor enjoyed being a traitor. I was quite certain that being a traitor did not trouble Caypor at all.

I finally made my decision. I was not sure why Caypor had become a spy for the Germans. For this reason I could not try to persuade him to spy for the British. I could not trust a man like Caypor. I knew also that his wife had a very strong influence[23] over him. I would never be able to persuade him to spy against the Germans. So somehow I had to persuade him to go over to England, to be shot. How would I do this? I had no idea.

POINTS FOR UNDERSTANDING

1. How did Ashenden know that Mrs Caypor hated him?
2. Did Ashenden think that Mrs Caypor had much influence over her husband?
3. What were the two sides of Caypor's character?
4. Why did Ashenden think that he would not be able to persuade Caypor to spy for the British?

7. A Walk with the Caypors

It was six days after my first German lesson. I had finished my evening meal in the dining-room, and was sitting outside the door of the hotel drinking a cup of coffee. Caypor came and sat next to me.

'My wife feels tired and she has gone upstairs to bed,' said Caypor with a friendly smile. 'Do you mind if I come and sit here with you?'

'No, not at all,' I answered. 'Sit down, please.'

He offered me a Swiss cigar. It was not a very good cigar, but I accepted it.

'I'm sorry I haven't got any better cigars,' said Caypor. 'Because of this war, you can't find good cigars. I must say that I'm tired of the war.'

I listened carefully. I felt that Caypor was going to talk about the war. I would let him talk so that I could learn as much as possible about his ideas. I would not say very much myself.

'My wife and I never talk about the war,' said Caypor. 'I'm very happy I can talk with you about it. I am sure that the Germans will lose the war, but I can't tell my wife that.'

Caypor obviously wanted me to believe what he was saying.

'Mhm,' I said. I answered like this because it could mean 'yes' or 'no'. Caypor might think that I was agreeing with him. He carried on talking.

'I feel so sad,' Caypor said. 'I cannot help England in this war. The English would not give me any job in the war because my wife is German. I tried to join the army, but they said I was too old. But I no longer enjoy living here in Switzerland. I must tell you that I want very much to do something for England. I know many languages, and I am sure I could be useful in the government department where you work.'

So this was why Caypor had come to talk to me. He wanted to find out more about the kind of work I did. I gave him some of the information I had already prepared with R. It was false, of course.

Caypor pulled his chair closer to mine, and lowered his voice.

'We don't want anyone to hear what we are saying,' he said softly. 'You know, the Swiss are very friendly with the Germans. But I'm sure you won't tell me any secrets.'

Then he told me one or two things which were secrets.

'I wouldn't tell anyone else but you,' he explained. 'I trust you.'

So I told him one or two more things. Again it was false information which I had prepared with R.

Caypor got up.

'You must excuse me,' he said to me, 'but my wife has already gone to bed. It is time for me to go, too. Thank you for the interesting conversation. Goodnight.'

I was sure that he was going to write a letter. He would pass on to the Germans all the information that I had just given him.

One Sunday, about a fortnight later, Caypor came to my table at breakfast.

'My wife and I are going on a little excursion²⁴,' he said. 'We are going for a walk up into the mountains. We will have lunch at a very nice restaurant. It is a fine day. If you feel strong enough, would you like to come with us? The walk and the air will do you good.'

'I should love to come with you,' I replied truthfully. 'I think I am strong enough to come on this excursion with you.'

The three of us set off together. I was prepared to enjoy the day with them; it was the first time I had gone far from the hotel since I had arrived. But I had to be careful. It was just possible that this was a trap. The Caypors might have discovered who I was. They might be taking me up into the mountains to kill me. I was sure that Mrs Caypor could do this. I remembered, too, that although Caypor was such a friendly person, he was also a traitor.

But Caypor seemed happy and relaxed. As we walked, he talked cheerfully all the time and told funny stories. I was surprised to see how much he knew about the mountain flowers. He could tell me the name of every flower we saw. Once he saw a pretty flower some way from our path. He went and picked it and came back to give it to his wife. I could see from his eyes that he loved the flower and he loved his wife.

'Isn't it a lovely flower?' he said to her.

Mrs Caypor looked at me.

'My husband likes flowers so much,' she said, 'I laugh at him sometimes. Often we have had almost no money. But even then he prefers to buy me flowers, although he should spend the money on food.'

I had sometimes seen Caypor come into the hotel with flowers in his hand, and give them to the old Irish lady. His interest in flowers was real. It showed a real kindness. I had always thought that flowers were uninteresting things. But Caypor talked about them in such a way that he made them sound interesting, even to me.

'You must have studied flowers a lot to know so much,' I said to him. 'Why don't you write a book about them?'

'I've never written a book,' he answered. 'There are too many books in the world. I have written a lot as a journalist, but that has always been for a newspaper. But if I stay in Switzerland much longer, I think I will write a book about the flowers of Switzerland. You should have been in Lucerne in the spring. The flowers were beautiful then.'

We reached the restaurant and sat down at a table outside. There was a lovely view of the lake below us and the mountains. We had a very nice lunch of fish which was fresh from the lake. We drank beer.

We all felt very pleased and happy with our excursion. Even Mrs Caypor was not so rude to me.

'In my heart I feel very happy now,' she said, 'even though such a terrible war is going on.'

There were tears in her eyes as she spoke.

Caypor took her hand and pressed it in his. I thought it best to leave them alone for a few minutes, so I walked to the other end of the restaurant garden. I looked at the view and thought again about Caypor and his wife, and Caypor's unusual character. I wondered too how I would get him to go to England. I still had no idea of how I was going to do this.

I must have been on my own for half an hour. Suddenly I heard a voice.

'There you are. We've been wondering where you were.'

It was Caypor. He and his wife were coming towards me. They were walking hand in hand. They looked at the view from the corner of the garden where I was.

'It's even more beautiful than the view where we were,' said Caypor. 'It's much better than being in England now with the war, isn't it?'

'Much,' I agreed with him.

'Did you have any difficulty in getting from England to Switzerland?' Caypor asked me.

'None at all. I had no trouble at the frontiers. As soon as they saw that I had an English passport, they let me cross the frontier immediately.'

I noticed Caypor look at his wife. I wondered why he looked at her. Perhaps Caypor was thinking how he could get to England. That would make my problem much easier. If Caypor himself really wanted to go to England, then I would not need to persuade him to go.

Before I could think any more about this, Mrs Caypor spoke.

'I think we had better start back soon for Lucerne.'

We walked back the way we had come, and reached the hotel after two hours.

POINTS FOR UNDERSTANDING

1. What did Caypor want to find out from Ashenden?
2. Why was it perhaps dangerous for Ashenden to go up the mountain with Mr and Mrs Caypor?
3. Why was Ashenden pleased when Caypor asked him about travelling from England to Switzerland?

8. Caypor Gets a Job

Two days later something unusual happened. It happened in the middle of a German lesson with Mrs Caypor.

'My husband has gone to Geneva today,' she said suddenly. 'He had some business to do there.'

'Oh,' I said. 'Will he be away for long?'

'No, only two days,' she replied.

I had the feeling that Mrs Caypor was telling a lie. I could not understand why she should suddenly tell me in the middle of a lesson that her husband had gone away. Why did she think that this would interest me? I thought that perhaps Caypor had not gone to Geneva at all, but to Berne. I knew that the German Intelligence Section had an office in Berne.

At lunch I talked to the waitress.

'You have a little less work to do today,' I said to her. 'I hear that Mr Caypor has gone to Berne.'

'Yes,' she replied. 'But he'll be back tomorrow.'

That did not prove for certain that Caypor had gone to Berne. But the waitress had not said that I was wrong. I sent a letter to a friend of mine in Berne, and asked him to find out if Caypor had been there.

The next evening Caypor came in for dinner with his wife. They did not speak to me. Caypor was not cheerful at all. They did not speak to each other at dinner time. They went straight to their rooms as soon as they had finished their meal.

The next morning I received a reply from my friend in Berne. He said that Caypor had been to Berne, and had been to the office of the German Intelligence Section.

I could guess what they had said to Caypor there. The Germans did not like paying him money for doing nothing in Lucerne. They were now going to send Caypor to England.

Of course, I was not certain of this. I was guessing again. But so often a spy must guess because he cannot ask people questions directly.

When Mrs Caypor came in to give me my lesson, she looked very tired. She did not seem willing to teach me. I guessed that she and her husband had been awake talking most of the night. I wondered what they had said. Did she try and persuade him to go to England or to stay in Switzerland?

She gave me a good lesson, but I could see that she was impatient. She wanted to finish the lesson quickly.

At lunch I watched them in the dining-room. Again they both looked worried and they hardly spoke to each other. They went out before I had finished. When I finished my meal and went out, I found Caypor sitting alone just outside the front door.

'Hello,' he said cheerfully. But I could see that he was finding it difficult to be cheerful. He did not find it easy to smile now.

'Come and have coffee with me,' he said. 'My poor wife has got a headache. I told her to go and lie down. She is rather worried, you see, because I am thinking of going to England.'

'Oh,' I said, showing interest. 'Will you be going for long?'

'The truth is,' said Caypor, 'that I am tired of doing nothing. I am afraid that the war will go on for many more years, and I can't stay here for ever. I think that the time has come for me to get a job. I may have a German wife, but I am an Englishman, and I want to help my country. Of course my wife is not happy with this idea.'

I could see a new look in Caypor's eyes; it was fear. Caypor was afraid. He did not want to go to England. He wanted to stay safely in Switzerland. I guessed what his boss had said to him in Berne. He had ordered Caypor to go to England.

I wondered if Caypor's wife had tried to persuade him to stay in Switzerland. I did not think so.

'Are you going to take your wife with you?' I asked him.

'No, she'll stay here,' he replied.

So I guessed that he would send information in his letters to her which would be useful to the Germans. Mrs Caypor would pass this information on to the German Intelligence.

Caypor turned to me.

'I've been away from England for so long,' he said. 'I don't know how I can find a job there. Can you help me?'

'I don't know,' I said. 'What kind of a job are you thinking of?'

'Well, I imagine I could do the same sort of job as you did,' Caypor replied. 'Is there anyone in your department who knows you well? You could write a letter to him saying that you have met me here in Switzerland. And you could give me the letter to take with me.'

I was very glad that Caypor was planning to go to England. I would no longer need to try and persuade him to go! He was going by himself.

'I could give you a note to the head of my department if you like,' I said. 'He knows me very well.'

'That would be excellent,' said Caypor.

'But of course I must tell the truth,' I warned him. 'I must say that I have only known you for about a fortnight.'

'Of course,' Caypor agreed. 'But you'll help me if you can, won't you?'

'Oh, certainly,' I said.

'I only hope that I can get a visa[25] to go to England,' said Caypor.

He got up suddenly.

'I must go and see how my wife is,' he said. 'When can you let me have that letter?'

'Whenever you like,' I replied. 'How soon are you leaving?'

'As soon as possible,' he said. 'Well, thank you for all the help you are going to give me.'

Caypor left me sitting there. I did not want to seem to be in a hurry, so I sat there for another ten minutes. Then I went upstairs. I had various letters to write.

First I prepared a letter to R. I told him that Caypor was going to England. The letter said, 'I am sending you the goods which you ordered.' R. would understand that by 'the goods' I meant Caypor. But if anyone else found the letter, they would not know what I meant.

Then I wrote to the British Consulate in Berne. I told them to give Caypor a visa if he asked for one. With a visa he could get into England without any difficulty.

The third letter was to the head of my department. This was the letter that Caypor had asked for. In my letter I said that I had known Caypor for a fortnight, but that I trusted him. I added that he should be given a job in the department if possible.

I sent off the first two letters. When I went in to dinner, I had Caypor's letter in my pocket. Caypor was not there, but when he came in a few minutes later, I gave him the letter.

POINTS FOR UNDERSTANDING
1. Why had Caypor gone to Berne?
2. Why did the Caypors look so worried the next morning?
3. How did Caypor ask Ashenden to help him?
4. What was Caypor going to do in England?
5. How many letters did Ashenden write and who were they written to?

9. Caypor in England

Two days later Caypor left for England.

Mrs Caypor remained in Lucerne, and I continued my lessons with her. Every morning after my lesson, I went to the post office to see if there were any letters for me. On the fourth day after Caypor had left, I had a letter from R. This letter told me that Caypor had just arrived in England.

I saw Mrs Caypor in the dining-room of the hotel an hour later.

'Have you had any news from your husband yet?' I asked her.

'No,' Mrs Caypor said. 'It's still early. I expect I will hear in the next day or two.'

Next day she was very impatient during the lesson. At the end of it, we both went to the post office. There was no letter for her and I knew that there never would be. She was very worried and upset.

'My husband promised to write from Paris,' she said. 'I am sure there must be a letter for me. But these people in the post office are stupid and they say there is no letter.'

I did not know what to say to her. She turned to the post office man.

'When do they bring you more letters?' she asked.

'About five o'clock this afternoon,' said the man.

'I'll come then,' said Mrs Caypor.

She went at five o'clock, but there was no letter for her. She was beginning to fear that something was wrong.

The next morning Mrs Caypor looked very ill. She must have been awake all night, worrying about her husband. She came to me at eleven o'clock.

'You must excuse me, Mr Somerville,' she said. 'I cannot give you a lesson. I am not feeling well.'

In the evening I got a note from Mrs Caypor. She said she was sorry, but she could not continue with the conversation lessons. She gave no reason. I did not see her for two days. She did not come down for meals. She only came out of her room twice a day and went straight to the post office.

I thought of Mrs Caypor sitting in her room, wondering what had happened to her husband. I began to feel a little sorry for her.

The next day I went to the post office again. I found

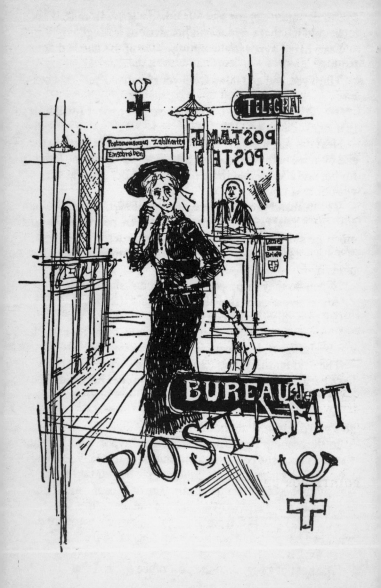

another letter for me from R. It said, 'Your latest order is being executed now.' It looked like an ordinary letter from a company. When a company writes, 'Your order is being executed,' it means 'we are sending you the goods which you have ordered.' But 'to execute somebody' can also mean to kill someone. And I knew that this was what had happened to Caypor.

While I was in the post office, Mrs Caypor came in. I was shocked to see how she looked. Her eyes looked very tired. She was as pale as death. She asked if there was a letter.

'I'm sorry, madam,' said the post office man, 'there's nothing yet.'

'But look, please look,' she said to the man at the post office. 'Are you sure there is no letter? Please look again.'

Her voice sounded frightened and nervous. The man took out all the letters again and looked through them.

'No, there's nothing, madam,' he said.

'Oh God,' she cried, 'oh God.'

She turned away with tears running down her tired face. For a moment she stood there, like a blind man who does not know which way to go.

Then a terrible thing happened. Fritzi the dog sat down, threw back his head and gave a long frightening cry.

Mrs Caypor looked at the dog. Her eyes seemed to come out of her head with fear. The terrible doubt of the past few days was no longer a doubt. She now knew what had happened to her husband. She knew she would never see her husband again because he was dead.

POINTS FOR UNDERSTANDING

1. Why did Mrs Caypor want a letter from her husband?
2. How did Ashenden know that Caypor was dead?
3. What made Mrs Caypor feel sure that her husband was dead?

Glossary

1. *gambler* – page 3
   a person who plays cards and other games in order to win money.

2. *diplomatic passport* – page 4
   a passport given to people who work abroad for their government. People with a diplomatic passport can go easily from one country to another.

3. *documents* – page 4
   papers with important facts or secret messages written on them.

4. *embassy* – page 4
   the offices of one country in a foreign country. Every country has embassies and consulates in all foreign countries. The embassy is usually in the capital and the consulates are in the seaports.

5. *at all costs* – page 5
   if you are told to do something at all costs, you must be ready to kill someone or be killed yourself in order to succeed.

6. *wig* – page 6
   false hair worn on the head. Many people who have no hair wear wigs.

7. *frontier, customs* – page 7
   the frontier is the place on a journey where you go from one country into another country. At the frontier you have to go through customs and show your passport to the customs officers. The customs officers can stop people from coming into their country. If the customs officers find someone with knives, guns, etc., they will stop him at the frontier. But they don't usually search the luggage of people with diplomatic passports.

8. *vain* – page 8
   somebody who is vain will spend a lot of time admiring his own clothes and appearance. He thinks that he is very important.

9. *stationmaster* – page 10
   the manager of a railway station. He is in charge of the other people who work at the station.

10. *scented water* – page 14
    water which has a sweet smell. People put scented water on their bodies and clothes to make them smell nice. Scent is the same as scented water.

11. *to change your mind* – page 16
    if you think that you like someone and, then, later you decide that you do not like that person, you have changed your mind.

12. *consulate* – page 19
    see gloss No. 4 – *embassy*

13. *damn* – page 24
    a word that people say to show that they are angry.

14. *boss* – page 27
    the person who you work for.

15. *embarrassed* – page 28
    made to feel uncomfortable and nervous because many people are looking at you.

16. *traitor* – page 35
    to betray – page 35
    a traitor is a spy who works for the enemy against his own country. A traitor betrays (works against) his own country.

17. *to confuse* – page 36
    to make someone unable to decide what is true and what is not true.

18. *to be suspicious (to suspect)* – page 37
    not to trust someone, because you think they are telling lies.

19. *government department* – page 38
    an office or group of offices in which people work for the government.

20. *couple* – page 40
    a man and a woman who are married to one another.

21. *to fall into a trap* – page 45
    to be tricked into doing something which will harm or hurt you.

22. *local dialect* – page 47
    a special way of speaking in one part of a country, which is not easily understood in any other part of the same country.

23. *influence* – page 55
    power. If you influence someone, he will do what you tell him.

24. *excursion* – page 57
    a visit which you make to another place for fun or pleasure.

25. *visa* – page 63
    permission stamped into your passport, to enter a country.

70

A Man From Glasgow and Mackintosh

A Man From Glasgow

On the nights when there is a full-moon
Morrison hears strange laughter.

Some people think that a full-moon
makes madmen excited.

But is Morrison mad?

Mackintosh

It started as a joke.

When Walker forced the villagers to build the road
and to pay for it, he thought it was funny.

It ended in death.

Books by W. Somerset Maugham (unsimplified)

LIZA OF LAMBETH
MRS. CRADDOCK
THE MAGICIAN
OF HUMAN BONDAGE
THE MOON AND SIXPENCE
THE TREMBLING OF A LEAF
ON A CHINESE SCREEN
THE PAINTED VEIL
THE CASUARINA TREE
ASHENDEN
THE GENTLEMAN IN THE PARLOUR
CAKES AND ALE
FIRST PERSON SINGULAR
THE NARROW CORNER
AH KING
DON FERNANDO
COSMOPOLITANS
THEATRE
THE SUMMING UP
CHRISTMAS HOLIDAY
BOOKS AND YOU
THE MIXTURE AS BEFORE
UP AT THE VILLA
STRICTLY PERSONAL
THE RAZOR'S EDGE
THEN AND NOW
CREATURES OF CIRCUMSTANCE
CATALINA
HERE AND THERE (*Collection of Short Stories*)
QUARTET (*Four Short Stories with Film Scripts*)
A WRITER'S NOTEBOOK
TRIO (*Three Short Stories with Film Scripts*)
THE COMPLETE SHORT STORIES (*3 vols.*)
ENCORE (*Three Short Stories with Film Scripts*)
THE VAGRANT MOOD
THE COLLECTED PLAYS (*3 vols.*)
THE SELECTED NOVELS (*3 vols.*)
THE PARTIAL VIEW
THE NOVELS AND THEIR AUTHORS
THE TRAVEL BOOKS